Original title:
Wrapped in Winter's Quilt

Copyright © 2024 Creative Arts Management OÜ
All rights reserved.

Author: Wyatt Kensington
ISBN HARDBACK: 978-9916-94-466-0
ISBN PAPERBACK: 978-9916-94-467-7

Layers of Chill and Comfort

Beneath the frost, the ground lies still,
A blanket white, a gentle thrill.
The air is crisp, a breath so pure,
Wrapped in warmth, we're safe, secure.

Each flake that falls, a soft embrace,
Nature's quilt, a tender space.
In layers thick, we hide away,
Where chill and comfort gently sway.

Cold Hands, Warm Hearts

Fingers numb from winter's bite,
Yet inside glows a fire bright.
Shared laughter warms the frosty night,
In whispered tones, our spirits ignite.

Though outside chills may make us sigh,
We gather close and never cry.
With cold hands held, we find our part,
For love can thaw the frost in heart.

Serene Stillness in White

A silent world, wrapped in white,
Soft snowflakes dance, pure and light.
The quiet hush, a gentle sound,
In this stillness, peace is found.

Trees wear coats of icy sheen,
Reflecting all, a tranquil scene.
In winter's grasp, we stop and stare,
As nature breathes, beyond compare.

Twilight in a Crystal Cocoon

As day gives way to night's embrace,
The world transforms, a mystic space.
Stars twinkle in the velvet deep,
In crystal light, the shadows creep.

The air is thick with magic's scent,
Within this cocoon, our thoughts are bent.
We dream beneath the frozen sky,
Where twilight whispers, soft and shy.

A Cocoon of Winter's Breath

Silent whispers fill the air,
Dreams enfolded, light as hair.
Softly wrapped in time's embrace,
Winter breathes in tranquil space.

Snowflakes dance in gentle flight,
Blanketing the world in white.
Nature rests, a quiet pause,
In the stillness, find the cause.

Branches bare yet strong remain,
Holding memories of the rain.
Stars twinkle in the brisk night sky,
Listening to the world's soft sigh.

Cocooned in a frosty shell,
Winter's song, a soothing bell.
Time to dream in peaceful glow,
Await the warmth that spring will show.

Hibernation of the Heart

In the silence, feelings grow,
Soft as shadows, deep below.
Whispers linger, thoughts in flight,
Longing echoes through the night.

Winter's chill wraps all in peace,
Moments pause, a sweet release.
Hearts retreat to cozy nooks,
Reading life in winter's books.

Outside, the world is cold and bare,
Yet inside, warmth holds us there.
Dreams weave softly, like a thread,
Hibernation, thoughts unsaid.

When the thaw breaks winter's song,
Hearts will wake, the wait was long.
For now, let the quiet reign,
In this hush, we can remain.

The Snow-Softened Earth

Underneath the blanket white,
Earth is quiet, hidden, slight.
Softly layered, winter's quilt,
All that's ancient, love is built.

Footprints fade in purest snow,
Nature whispers, soft and slow.
Fields now rest, their stories pause,
Offering a silent applause.

Gentle flakes on branches cling,
Trimming trees in frozen bling.
Every corner wrapped with care,
Time to breathe, a moment rare.

Though the world may seem so still,
Life stirs gently, heart and will.
Soon the thaw will warm the earth,
But for now, behold its birth.

Traces of Frost on Forgotten Paths

Footsteps lost along the way,
Paths once clear now fade to gray.
Frosty patterns map the ground,
Stories whisper, barely found.

Through the trees, the chill winds blow,
Marking trails where few may go.
Nature holds her secrets tight,
In the silence, day to night.

Cold embraces, yet it speaks,
Of the hope that winter seeks.
Every breath is crystal clear,
Traces linger, drawing near.

As the thaw begins to swell,
Memories of frost will tell.
Paths once lost will soon be bright,
Guided gently by the light.

Frosted Memories Unraveled

Whispers of frost touch the air,
Echoes of laughter everywhere.
Footsteps lost in a snow-white haze,
Haunting the heart, in frozen plays.

Crystals dance in the waning light,
Reflections of joy, a bittersweet sight.
Forgotten dreams in the softest glow,
Faded by time, yet still they flow.

The Comfort of Cold Embrace

Beneath a blanket of purest white,
Hope finds warmth on a frigid night.
Each flake whispers tales of yore,
In the silence, we yearn for more.

Breath visible in the crisp, still air,
Moments shared, a secret pair.
Wrapped in solace, winter's delight,
Holding close till the first light.

Beneath the Winter's Solace

Stars peek down through the frosted trees,
Softly kissed by the biting breeze.
A hush descends on the sleeping ground,
In winter's arms, tranquility found.

Sleds and laughter carve out paths,
Fleeting joy in the chilly drafts.
Beneath the moon's tender gaze,
Hearts entwine in the winter's maze.

Portraits in White

Brushstrokes of snow paint the scene,
Canvas of dreams in a winter sheen.
Each flurry captures a moment passed,
In the gallery of memories, vast.

Figures etched in a crystal glow,
Stories written that none will know.
In the silence of winter's might,
Lives immortalized, portraits in white.

The Elegance of Frost

Delicate patterns lace the glass,
A silent artistry at dawn's pass.
Fingers touch, they shiver and cling,
Nature's beauty, a winter's fling.

Breathtaking hues in morning light,
Whispers of magic whispering bright.
Each crystal glistens, pure and clear,
In frosty breath, the world draws near.

Moonlit Glimmers on Snow

Beneath the stars, the snowflakes gleam,
In silver light, the night's sweet dream.
A tranquil hush blankets the land,
With every heartbeat, silence grand.

Footprints vanish in the moon's glow,
Echoes of whispers, soft and slow.
In this moment, the world is still,
Captured in magic, hearts to fill.

Shadows of the Longest Night

The dark surrounds, yet sparks ignite,
Whispers of secrets held in the night.
Shadows dance in soft twilight,
Holding stories within their flight.

Candle flames flicker, a warm embrace,
Illuminating this hidden space.
In silence, dreams begin to weave,
In shadows linger, tales we believe.

Cozy Aromas in the Chill

Hot cocoa brews, the steam entwines,
A comforting warmth, the heart defines.
Cinnamon swirls and nutmeg tease,
Creating a haven, a sweet appease.

As frost nips at each window pane,
Fireside tales wash away the pain.
Wrapped in blankets, laughter flows,
In cozy aromas, love surely grows.

Twinkling Stars Beneath Frost

In a blanket of silver, the night does weave,
Stars like whispers within the freeze.
Glisten and shimmer through the icy air,
Each one a promise, a dream to share.

Silent the world beneath the endless sky,
Moonlight dances, as shadows lie.
Frost-kissed branches, glittering bright,
Holding the secrets of the winter night.

Hearthside Reflections

Gathered around where the warmth draws near,
Laughter and stories, the joys we share.
Embers flicker, with a soft embrace,
In the glow of our hearth, we find our place.

Winter winds howl through the chilly air,
But here by the fire, we banish despair.
Each tale a thread in the fabric spun,
Under the spell of the setting sun.

The Stillness of Winter's Night

Blanketed white, the world lies still,
Time pauses gently, as if by will.
Wrapped in silence, the moon claims the sky,
Nature's soft whispers, a lullaby.

Footsteps muffled on the powdery ground,
In this quiet moment, peace can be found.
Stars peek shyly, like eyes full of grace,
In the stillness of night, we find our place.

Enchanted in Arctic Hues

Colors emerge in the cold, crisp air,
Blues and purples danced with flair.
The northern lights shimmer, a tapestry bright,
Illuminating dreams in the depths of night.

Icicles hang like jewels from eaves,
A spell cast softly among the leaves.
In this arctic wonderland, hearts entwine,
Lost in the magic, so pure and divine.

Beneath the Silver Shroud

The moonlight dances on the snow,
Casting shadows, soft and low.
Whispers carried on the breeze,
Nature's secrets, a gentle tease.

Trees stand tall, adorned in white,
Guardians of this tranquil night.
Footsteps crunch on frozen ground,
A world of magic all around.

Stars peek through the silver haze,
Guiding lost souls through the maze.
In this stillness, hearts find grace,
As time slows down, we hold our place.

Beneath the shroud, we dream anew,
Wrapped in wonder, me and you.
A moment carved from winter's breath,
In this silence, we embrace depth.

Snowflakes in Soft Embrace

Falling gently from the sky,
Snowflakes swirl as if to fly.
Each one unique, a fleeting kiss,
A moment wrapped in winter's bliss.

They blanket fields in purest white,
Transforming day into the night.
Whispers of the cold arrive,
In their presence, we feel alive.

Laughter echoes in the chill,
Children's joy is never still.
Snowmen stand with coal for eyes,
Underneath the wintry skies.

As the world slows to a crawl,
Snowflakes dance, a gentle call.
In their soft embrace, we find,
A solace for the heart and mind.

The Silent Serenade

In the stillness of the night,
A serenade devoid of light.
The stars above begin to sing,
To the night, their secrets cling.

Silence wraps the earth in peace,
From chaos, we find sweet release.
Moonbeams shimmer on the lake,
In this moment, hearts awake.

Winds caress the branches bare,
A lullaby floats through the air.
Nature's hymn, a soft refrain,
Echoing through the night's domain.

In the quiet, dreams take flight,
Embraced by the softest light.
As dawn approaches, shadows fade,
In the silence, love is made.

Embracing the Icy Night

The night unfolds with icy breath,
Chilled whispers dance, a waltz with death.
Stars twinkle like diamonds bright,
Illuminating the velvet night.

Frost-kissed trees in moonlit glow,
Stand like sentinels, row on row.
A symphony of silence sings,
With peace that only winter brings.

Footsteps echo on the street,
In the stillness, hearts can beat.
Wrapped in warmth, we find our place,
Embracing winter's cool embrace.

While the world sleeps, dreams ignite,
In the calm of this icy night.
Together, we gaze at the sky,
Underneath the stars up high.

Beneath the Canvas of Winter

Snowflakes dance in gentle bliss,
Painting hush on earth's soft kiss.
Branches bare in silent grace,
Nature wears a calm embrace.

Footsteps crunch on icy ground,
Whispers echo all around.
Every breath a fleeting sigh,
Winter's winds like dreams drift by.

Stars reflect on frozen streams,
Cloaked in silver, glimmering dreams.
Night descends with velvet cloak,
In its arms, our spirits soak.

Beneath this canvas, pure and white,
Hearts find solace, lost in light.
In the stillness, time stands still,
Peace surrounds with every chill.

Cold Breath of the Dawn

Morning breaks with icy breath,
A shiver runs, a dance with death.
Shadows flee from day's bright eye,
Clouds embrace the waking sky.

Frosted grass, a crystal sheen,
Nature's jewels, pure and keen.
Birdsong weaves through chilly air,
A promise blooms, beyond despair.

With every ray, the world ignites,
Echoes of warm, forgotten nights.
Hope unfurls, a tender flower,
In the cold pale of this hour.

Yet here we stand, hearts wise and bold,
In cold embrace, new stories told.
Each dawn whispers what we seek,
Life awakens, soft yet sleek.

Frosted Threads of Memory

Whispers wrapped in muted sound,
Frosted threads of past unbound.
In the chill, old echoes hum,
Stories fade, but never numb.

Each flake falls like gentle tears,
Carving paths through hidden fears.
Moments frozen, time's allure,
In the hush, old hearts feel pure.

Voices linger, soft and sweet,
In the air where shadows meet.
Silent prayers upon the breeze,
Captured dreams among the trees.

Through the winter's breath we roam,
Finding solace, a hidden home.
In frosted threads, our lives entwine,
Through the cold, memories shine.

Quiet Hours Beneath the Icicles

Beneath the drape of icy light,
Whispers flow through the quiet night.
Icicles hang like crystal tears,
Marking time of fleeting years.

In this moment, calm and still,
Nature rests, the heart can fill.
Glimmers fade in soft twilight,
Silent vows beneath the night.

Fires crackle, warmth to chase,
Dancing shadows, love's embrace.
Together lost in winter's hold,
Stories shared, new and old.

As stars appear and silence reigns,
In quiet hours, love remains.
Underneath these icicles bright,
Hearts unite within the night.

The Gentle Weight of Ice

The world lies still beneath a sheet,
Soft whispers curl in frozen air.
Each flake a dream, a crystal sweet,
Holding secrets, unaware.

Branches bow with silver shrouds,
While shadows stretch in fading light.
Nature drapes her silent crowds,
In the hush of winter's night.

Footsteps crunch on frosty ground,
Echoes drift like fading sighs.
In the stillness, peace is found,
Beneath the vast, unclouded skies.

Beneath the weight, the heart beats slow,
As time itself seems to unfold.
In this beauty, warmth will grow,
A story waiting to be told.

Slumbering Under the Icebound Starlight

Stars caress the slumbering earth,
With soft glows that dance and play.
In the quiet, there's a birth,
Of dreams that drift and fade away.

The moon hangs low, a lantern bright,
Casting beams on frozen streams.
In this calm, ensnared by night,
Whispers linger like sweet dreams.

Trees stand tall, in silence dressed,
Encased in crystal, time stands still.
In winter's hold, they find their rest,
As hearts await the spring's warm thrill.

Underneath the icy glow,
Life lies waiting, wrapped in peace.
A gentle sigh, a soft hello,
In the stillness, troubles cease.

The Solitude of Shivered Branches

In the forest, branches shiver,
Clothed in frost, a glistening gown.
Silent whispers, a muted river,
As the snowflakes softly drown.

Each twig an echo, brittle, bare,
Framed against the fading light.
In their stillness, a quiet prayer,
Hoping for the return of night.

The weight of silence softly speaks,
To those who wander, lost in thought.
Where solitude, like winter, seeks,
The warmth of solace dearly caught.

Nature's breath, a misty sigh,
Drifting through the bitter cold.
Underneath a slate-gray sky,
Lies the beauty yet untold.

Dreams in a Snowscape

In a realm of white, dreams awaken,
Frosted fields cradle the night.
Each snowflake a story unshaken,
Woven with whispers of light.

The horizon stretches, pure and wide,
Where shadows dance in soft reprieve.
Under the moon, the world does hide,
In layers of dreams meant to weave.

Footsteps in the snow are fleeting,
Leaving prints like memories grand.
In this realm, my heart's retreating,
Finding solace in a wonderland.

A canvas brushed in winter's hue,
Where visions twirl in graceful loops.
In this snowscape, fresh and new,
I gather dreams like gentle ghoups.

A Tidal Silence of Winter

In the hush of the evening light,
Snow blankets the world, pure and white.
Whispers weave through the frigid air,
Nature's secrets, laid gently bare.

Footprints mark a journey's start,
Each step echoes, a work of art.
Branches bow with a heavy load,
Silent stories along the road.

Stars glimmer in the frosty night,
Casting spells with their silver light.
The calmness wraps like a soft shawl,
In this winter's embrace, we stand tall.

As tides of silence drift and sway,
Winter breathes in a tranquil way.
Moments frozen, yet time moves on,
In the stillness, a soft new dawn.

Comfort in the Cold

Beneath a quilt of icy sheets,
Lies warmth in the heart where love greets.
Cocoa brews by the fireside glow,
As winter winds whisper and blow.

Toasty socks and a hearty stew,
Embrace the chill, let joy ensue.
This season wraps us in its hold,
Crafting tales to be cherished bold.

Carols sung in a frosted night,
Voices mingle in pure delight.
From window panes, the world looks bright,
In cozy corners, we find our light.

Though storms may howl and snow may fall,
In each other, we stand tall.
The cold may bite, but hearts stay warm,
Together we shelter from any storm.

Frost's Gentle Kiss

Morning breaks with a frosty breath,
The earth adorned in a delicate sheath.
Each blade of grass, a crystal gem,
Whispers of frost, nature's diadem.

Clouds of white drift against the blue,
A canvas painted, fresh and new.
The sun dances on frozen streams,
Awakening life from winter's dreams.

Gentle winds carry a chilly bite,
Yet warmth ignites in the softest light.
Frost glistens like diamonds on trees,
A world transformed with effortless ease.

In this season of tranquil grace,
We find our place in this serene space.
Frost's gentle kiss, a sweet embrace,
Nature's wonder, an endless chase.

Calendar of Frosted Moments

Each month unveils a frosted scene,
A winter's tale, crisp and clean.
January sparkles with icy cheer,
While February whispers, love draws near.

March brings hints of springtime's breath,
Yet still we linger, savoring the depth.
April's showers soften the chill,
As frost retreats, the world starts to fill.

May dances in a gentle hue,
With memories of frost, so few.
The year unfolds in cycles of time,
Each moment captured in rhythm and rhyme.

Through seasons' turn, we hold each day,
A calendar etched in a pure display.
Frosted moments form the year's art,
Each snapshot cherished, close to the heart.

The Frosted Labyrinth

In the quiet of winter's grip,
A labyrinth of frost does creep.
Each path, a fleeting memory,
In the stillness, secrets sleep.

Branches clad in icy lace,
Whispers echo, a ghostly trace.
Footsteps lost in shards of light,
Guided by the pale moon's face.

Snow-Cloaked Whispers of the Past

Softly falls the winter snows,
Blanketing what time forgot.
In silence, hidden stories lie,
Joy and sorrow interwrought.

Each flake, a tale from days of yore,
Whispers drift as memories soar.
Through the chill, a warmth remains,
In the heart, the past implores.

Coalescing into the Night's Embrace

Stars entwine in velvet skies,
Veils of darkness softly spill.
Every breath a silent song,
As dreams merge with the night's chill.

The moon, a guardian so bright,
Cradles all within her light.
Shadows dance in gentle sway,
Coalescing, they fade from sight.

A Hearth of Forgotten Stories

By the fire, stories untold,
Embers flicker, a warm glow.
Voices murmur of days gone by,
In the hearth, the past does flow.

Memories breathe, ignite the flame,
Each tale woven, none the same.
In shadows cast, the laughter lingers,
A tapestry of love, no shame.

Stillness of Snowfall Reverie

In the hush of night, snowflakes descend,
Whispers of silence, where dreams blend.
A world wrapped in white, soft and pure,
Each flake a story, delicate and sure.

Branches are cloaked in a blanket of grace,
Time slows its march in this tranquil space.
Footprints forgotten, secrets unfold,
Magic and wonder in the stillness told.

The Enfolding Hues of Winter

Beneath the gray sky, a palette appears,
With strokes of white, melting all fears.
Crimson and cedar, the colors ignite,
A canvas of warmth in the coldest night.

The trees stand tall, a guardianship grand,
Embroidered in frost, a shimmering band.
Nature's own art, in stillness it sings,
Winter's embrace, the solace it brings.

Chasing Shadows through the Snow

In twilight's glow, shadows dance and weave,
A playful pursuit, make-believe.
Footsteps echo, laughter in the air,
Chasing the whispers, a game so rare.

Every turn brings a secret to find,
Snow-covered trails, uncharted and blind.
The world is alive in the soft, moonlight,
Chasing shadows through the wintry night.

A Tapestry of Ice and Light

Crystal creations in the dawn's early glow,
Nature's own jewels in the shimmering show.
Reflecting the sun, they shimmer and gleam,
In a tapestry woven from the winter's dream.

Icicles hang like delicate lace,
Framing the windows of this frosty place.
An ephemeral beauty, fleeting and bright,
A dance of the seasons in ice and light.

The Quietude of Falling Flakes

Softly they dance, in silence they drift,
Whispers of winter, a delicate gift.
Each flake a secret, softly it glows,
Unraveling stories, as the cold wind blows.

Blanketing earth with a hush sublime,
Nature's soft breath, a rhythm in rhyme.
Children's laughter breaks the still air,
In the quietude, magic is rare.

Stars peek through, adorned in their frost,
Moments of stillness, never quite lost.
A world transformed, in white it remains,
Beauty in stillness, joy in the chains.

Under the moon, a tableau so fine,
Falling like feather, divine and benign.
In this embrace, all troubles subside,
The quietude whispers, with peace as our guide.

Beneath the Crystal Canopy

Beneath the branches, glittering bright,
A crystal canopy, pure winter light.
Twinkling like diamonds, the world is aglow,
In this enchanting, serene tableau.

Footsteps are muffled, the air crisp and clear,
Upon frosty paths, the heart feels no fear.
Nature's soft hush, a gentle embrace,
Whispers of magic in this sacred space.

Icicles hang like elegant dreams,
Draped from the roof, in delicate seams.
Shadows are dancing, as day starts to fade,
Beneath the canopy, memories are made.

Embraced by silence, a moment so rare,
Beneath the branches, worries lay bare.
In tranquility's arms, the spirit will soar,
Beneath the crystal, we'll always want more.

Seasons' Gentle Lullaby

Winter's embrace in the dark of the night,
A lullaby whispers, tranquil and light.
Snowflakes are falling, weaving their song,
In the chill of the night, where dreams belong.

Spring taps softly, with buds breaking free,
A melody rising, so sweetly we see.
Gentle the breezes, igniting new flame,
In the seasons' choirs, no two notes the same.

Summer's warmth glows in laughter untold,
A bright serenade as the world turns bold.
The sun plays its notes, on wings it will fly,
In the heart of the warmth, seasons comply.

Autumn arrives with its rich, rustling leaves,
A tapestry woven as twilight weaves.
In shades of amber, the earth starts to sigh,
Embracing the cycle, the seasons comply.

Tranquility of Icy Nights

In icy embrace, the world holds its breath,
A stillness pervades, a dance with death.
Stars shimmer bright, on blankets of snow,
In tranquility's arms, we quietly flow.

Moonlight it weaves through the branches bare,
Casting soft shadows, a tranquil affair.
The air bites gently, yet hearts feel no pain,
In whispers of night, peace falls like the rain.

Crystals adorning the edges of time,
Frozen in beauty, a soft, silent chime.
Dreams intertwining in slumber's sweet hold,
In icy cocoon, all stories unfold.

Time stands still under the celestial dome,
Each heartbeat echoes, a feeling of home.
In the tranquility, all worries fade right,
Embraced by the magic of icy nights.

Frosted Embrace

In the stillness of the night,
Whispers of ice take flight.
Branches draped in silver hue,
Nature's quiet, crisp debut.

Footsteps crunch on frozen ground,
Echoes of the silence found.
Stars above like diamonds bright,
Guide us through the frosty light.

The breath of winter fills the air,
Each exhale, a frosted flare.
Wrapped in warmth, we stand close,
In this chill, we find our most.

Hearts aglow with tender fire,
Holding close what we desire.
In this frosted, sweet embrace,
Time stands still, a sacred space.

The Silent Blanket

Snowflakes gently fall from sky,
A soft whisper, a silent sigh.
Blanketing the earth in white,
Transforming day into soft night.

Houses nod with roofs adorned,
Windows glow, the hearths are warmed.
Children laugh, their joy unfurled,
In the magic of this world.

Each flake tells a story rare,
Drifting softly through the air.
Nature sleeps, profound and deep,
Underneath the silence, peace.

As day turns bright, the sun will gleam,
Melting down our winter dream.
Yet in memory, it remains,
The silent blanket, winter's reign.

Beneath Winter's Veil

Beneath a veil of glistening frost,
Life finds beauty, never lost.
Each branch in white, a canvas bare,
Breath of winter fills the air.

Shadows dance beneath the trees,
Carried softly by the breeze.
Muffled sounds and tender light,
Guide us through this frozen night.

The world in slumber, dreams secure,
Whispers of magic endure.
Nature holds its breath so still,
Prepared for warmth, when time will thrill.

With each dawn, a promise made,
Tales of spring in silence laid.
Yet beneath this icy shroud,
Life waits patiently, unbowed.

Chilling Whispers of Snow

Chilling whispers fill the air,
As snowflakes dance without a care.
Frosted kisses on my skin,
In this winter, magic spins.

The world adorned in crystal dreams,
Sparkling bright as daylight beams.
Footprints trace a path of light,
Leading onward through the night.

Voices fade, the stillness hums,
Nature pauses, peace becomes.
Each flake falls like a gentle sigh,
Covering earth, as time slips by.

Together wrapped in warmth and glow,
We wander through the chilling snow.
In this beauty, we will find,
The whispers freeze, yet hearts are kind.

Threads of Ice and Warmth

In the hush of winter's night,
Frosted breath glimmers bright,
Threads of ice weave and twine,
While warmth in hearts aligns.

Silent whispers fill the air,
Snowflakes dance without a care,
Embers glow, a soft embrace,
In this tranquil, sacred space.

Beneath the stars, we find our way,
Finding peace in night and day,
Threads connecting, strong yet thin,
A tapestry of loss and win.

Through the chill, our spirits soar,
Each moment shared—what we adore,
In the weave of ice and heat,
Life's great tapestry's complete.

Hibernating Dreams

In the stillness, shadows creep,
Winter's blanket, cold and deep,
Dreams of spring, so far away,
Nature rests, at peace to stay.

Beneath the frost, life lies still,
Waiting for the sun to fill,
The world with warmth, a gentle sigh,
As time drifts slowly by.

Creatures nestled, snug and tight,
In their burrows, out of sight,
Whispers of the dreams they share,
While the chill hangs in the air.

Soon the world will wake anew,
Sunlight's kiss imbued with dew,
But for now, we close our eyes,
Hibernating 'neath the skies.

The Coziness of Cold

Blankets wrapped, a hearth aglow,
Outside, the icy winds do blow,
Within these walls, we sit and smile,
The coziness, we know, worth our while.

Teacups steaming, laughter rings,
A moment shared, oh how it clings,
Each sip warms, as stories unfold,
In our hearts, against the cold.

The fire crackles, shadows dance,
In winter's grasp, we take a chance,
To cherish each laugh, each sigh,
As outside snowflakes gently fly.

Through frosty panes, we watch it fall,
A wondrous dream, enchanting all,
In the chill, our spirits rise,
Finding warmth, where love lies.

Frosted Tales by Firelight

Gather close, the fire's bright,
Casting shadows, pure delight,
Frosted tales begin to flow,
As the winter winds all blow.

With every crackle and each word,
Magic stirs, the heart is stirred,
In the glow, our fears take flight,
Embracing warmth, the chilling night.

Stories of heroes, lost and brave,
Of icy paths that hearts can save,
Each tale woven with care and thread,
In this moment, all else spread.

When the night fades into dawn,
And with it, frosted tales are gone,
Yet in our hearts, they will remain,
Echoes of warmth in winter's reign.

Layers of Silence Under Snow

Softly the snow blankets the ground,
Covering whispers with each gentle mound.
Footsteps are hushed in the frosty air,
Nature's stillness beyond compare.

Beneath the white lies a world asleep,
Promises hidden in silence deep.
Every flake dances in a silent show,
In the layers of silence, secrets grow.

Branches sag low with a crystal sheen,
Guarding the quiet, serene and clean.
Time seems to pause under winter's reign,
In this moment, calmness remains.

Ghosts of the past wrapped in pure white,
Memories linger in the fading light.
As dawn awakens with a blush of gold,
The layers of silence begin to unfold.

The Art of Winter's Stillness

In the heart of winter, where time stands still,
Nature crafts calm with a delicate will.
Frost-kissed branches reach for the sky,
Painting a canvas as the days drift by.

Snowflakes twirl like dancers in flight,
Whispering secrets throughout the night.
Each crystal a story, a moment in time,
An artful display, both simple and prime.

The hush of the world wraps around me tight,
Comfort in shadows, warmth in the night.
Every breath taken in the cold, pure air,
Is a piece of winter's quiet affair.

As daylight breaks over the distant hill,
The art of stillness continues to thrill.
In the chill of the season, I find my peace,
A moment of magic, a sweet release.

Ghosts of Chill Past

Whispers of winter linger in the breeze,
Echoes of footsteps beneath barren trees.
Frosted memories dance through the night,
The ghosts of chill past fade out of sight.

Crystals adorn the world in a shroud,
An icy silence wraps the earth like a cloud.
Laughter of ages, lost to the frost,
In the chill of history, so much is tossed.

Reflections shimmer on a frozen lake,
Tales of the brave, of love, and heartbreak.
Each breath I take carries a trace,
Of moments long gone, in this magical space.

With every snowfall, the stories revive,
Breathing new life into what we derive.
Ghosts of chill past, we'll never forget,
In the heart of winter, they linger yet.

Whispers Across the Glacial Field

Across the glacial field, secrets reside,
Whispers of ancients where shadows abide.
Ice flows like rivers, glistening bright,
Holding the essence of day and night.

Silent stories told in crystal form,
Echoes of nature, both calm and warm.
Every crackling sound, a tale to share,
In the vastness of cold, we breathe in the air.

The stillness is loud, a haunting refrain,
Touching the soul, like a soft, gentle rain.
Under the blue, where the horizon meets,
Whispers carry forth on the chilly beats.

In the heart of winter, we find our place,
In the glacial field, we seek and embrace.
Through every whisper, in silence we find,
The beauty of winter, and peace of mind.

Nightfall in a Shimmering Blanket

The sky blends with shades of deep blue,
Stars emerge, one by one, anew.
A blanket of silence drapes the land,
As shadows stretch by night's command.

Moonlight dances on silver sea,
Whispers of dreams in harmony.
Each breath taken, crisp and clear,
The world asleep, drawing near.

Crickets sing their evening tune,
While gentle breezes softly croon.
The darkness holds a tender grace,
In this stillness, a warm embrace.

Nightfall wraps the earth so tight,
In shimmering darkness, pure delight.
Close your eyes and drift away,
Into the magic of the gray.

Dreams of a Snowbound World

A diamond quilt adorns the ground,
In silence, beauty knows no bound.
Trees draped in white, a heavenly sight,
Create a kingdom, pure and bright.

Footprints soft in powdery snow,
Silent tales of where we go.
Whispers carried by the frost,
In this realm, we gain, not lost.

Children laugh, in pure delight,
Snowballs flying, hearts so light.
Every flake a fleeting kiss,
In this landscape, find your bliss.

As night descends, the stars take flight,
Cloaked in peace, this world feels right.
Dreams of warmth amid the cold,
In this snowbound tale, love unfolds.

The Stillness Between Storms

A hush prevails in the fragile air,
Nature pauses, as if aware.
Clouds gather, gray and low,
Yet stillness reigns, time moves slow.

Birds seek shelter, quiet their song,
In this moment, the calm feels long.
Branches sway with gentle ease,
A breath held back, a whispered plea.

Lightning flickers on the horizon,
The calm before, a mysterious surprise on,
The world awaits the wild embrace,
Of winds that whip with fierce grace.

In this stillness, all senses peak,
A fleeting peace, words left to speak.
Hold onto the quiet, let it last,
Amidst the chaos, memories cast.

Snow-Flecked Memories

Snowflakes swirl like thoughts in mind,
Fleeting moments we seek to find.
Each flake a whisper of times gone by,
In winter's grasp, we laugh and sigh.

Frozen breaths, shared with glee,
Starlit paths that set us free.
Footprints linger on the white,
Echoes of warmth, soft and bright.

Childhood moments, crisp in air,
Snowman smiles and friendly care.
Hot cocoa warm in ready hands,
In snowy dreams, love understands.

As memories drift like flakes in sky,
Time weaves stories that never die.
Each winter's tale, a gentle touch,
Snow-flecked moments, we cherish much.

Hearth's Glow in Winter's Grasp

In the quiet night, flames flicker bright,
Shadows dance and play in warm, golden light.
Outside, the snow falls soft and white,
Within, the heart feels snug and right.

Family gathered, stories unfold,
Each crackle of wood, a memory told.
In the glow of the hearth, we find our hold,
A bond greater than silver or gold.

Mugs of cocoa, steam rising high,
Laughter echoes as time passes by.
Wrapped in blankets, we sigh a sigh,
In this cozy haven, we let worries die.

The winter winds howl, but here we stay,
Nestled together, come what may.
With love as our shield against the fray,
In the hearth's warm glow, we find our way.

Frost-Kissed Whispers

Underneath the moon's soft, pale glow,
The world lies still, wrapped in white snow.
Whispers of frost in the breezes flow,
Secrets of winter, they quietly show.

Trees dressed in crystals, a shimmering sight,
Branches like lace against the night.
Each breath we take brings frosty delight,
In the silence, we marvel at nature's might.

Footsteps crunch on the icy path,
Launching quiet thoughts, invoking a laugh.
In this stillness, we find warmth's aftermath,
Held in the beauty of winter's photograph.

Stars twinkle above, twirling dreams alive,
In the cold's embrace, our spirits thrive.
Nature whispers secrets, together we strive,
In frost-kissed moments, we are revived.

Beneath the Snowy Veil

Under a blanket of shimmering white,
Life slows down in the soft, quiet night.
Each flake that falls, a delicate sight,
Creating a canvas pristine and bright.

Footprints are hidden, silence takes hold,
Stories of seasons in whispers unfold.
The world seems softer, a beauty so bold,
Wrapped beneath snow, in dreams we behold.

Branches laden, trees bow low,
In this serene moment, the heartbeats slow.
Time stands still as the winter winds blow,
Beneath the snowy veil, peace starts to grow.

A blanket of calm, the world dressed anew,
In the hush of the night, dreams drift through.
With each quiet moment, a chance to renew,
Under the snowy veil, our spirits pursue.

Chilled Embrace of Solitude

In the frosty air, silence surrounds,
Echoes of thoughts, in stillness abound.
Outside, the world wears a cold, white gown,
Inside, a warmth where peace can be found.

Alone in the glow of a flickering flame,
Every shadow whispers a comforting name.
In solitude's arms, we're safe just the same,
Finding strength in stillness, no need for acclaim.

Windows frost over, a breath of the past,
Moments of quiet, too precious to last.
In the chill of the night, the peace is vast,
In solitude's embrace, we find joy unsurpassed.

Here, in the quiet, we learn to be free,
In the chill of the night, a heart's melody.
With every soft breath, we seek harmony,
In solitude's space, our souls find their glee.

Fables of the Frosted Ether

In whispers cold, the stories dwell,
Of frozen dreams, where shadows swell.
A glimmer bright, on winter's breath,
Tales woven softly, beneath the chest.

The trees tell secrets, dressed in white,
While nighttime stars, twinkle in sight.
In the stillness, magic stirs,
Echoing through the frozen furs.

With every flake, a narrative spun,
Lost in the hush, where time is undone.
The frost holds truths, ancient and wise,
In the quiet realm, where silence lies.

Come, gather near the frosted brook,
Dive into tales that beg for a look.
In the chilled embrace, let legends flow,
In fables of frost, our hearts shall grow.

Silence Beneath the Snow-Drift

Silent layers drape the earth,
Whispers hushed, embrace their worth.
Beneath the drift, secrets remain,
Cradled gently, in soft, white grain.

The moon hangs low, in tranquil grace,
Illuminating this quiet space.
A blanket thick, of quiet peace,
In snow's embrace, all troubles cease.

Footsteps muffled in frozen air,
The world outside, a distant care.
Nature pauses, time stands still,
In silent moments, find our will.

Beneath the snow, a warmth resides,
Where dreams take root and hope abides.
In the stillness, our hearts connect,
In silence found, we reflect.

Embraced by the Frost

Wrapped in whispers of icy lace,
Frosted kisses, nature's embrace.
Each crystal gem, a tale to share,
In the chill of night, we find our care.

Beneath the stars, the world aglow,
Wrapped in blankets of purest snow.
In winter's arms, we are set free,
With every breath, a melody.

Branches sway with a gentle sigh,
Where frozen moments never die.
Every heartbeat, the frosty tune,
Guided softly by the bright moon.

In the quiet, we find our song,
As winter whispers, we belong.
Embraced by frost, our spirits soar,
In this chill, we yearn for more.

Tucked in a Shroud of Snow

Tucked in layers of glittering white,
The earth lies still, bathed in night.
Each flake a memory, crisp and pure,
In winter's hold, we find our cure.

Blanketed dreams, soft and deep,
Cradled gently, lost in sleep.
A world transformed, by nature's hand,
In silence, we rise, as dreams expand.

In the hush, our worries fade,
Beneath the snow, a promise laid.
The frosty breath of winter's grace,
In every drift, we find our place.

Tucked away in a silent realm,
Where hope and joy are at the helm.
In snow's embrace, we stand and grow,
In this paradise, tucked in the snow.

Hearthside Dreams

Flickering flames in the night,
Whispers of warmth take flight.
Gentle shadows dance and sway,
In this cozy, golden bay.

Memories wrapped in soft glow,
Stories shared, the heart will sow.
Laughter mingles with the heat,
Each heartbeat, a rhythmic beat.

Outside, the world is cold and bare,
But here, love lingers in the air.
A haven where our spirits rise,
Beneath the stars, we dream and sigh.

Together we weave our quiet night,
Cradled in the firelight bright.
Hearthside dreams, a sweet embrace,
Time stands still in this safe place.

A Blanket of White Silence

Fallen flakes on silent ground,
Whispers of peace can be found.
Nature's quilt of purest white,
Blanketing the world so bright.

Footsteps muffled, a soft tread,
Each breath creates a frosty spread.
Trees adorned in crystal lace,
Holding winter's gentle grace.

In the stillness, dreams take flight,
Stars peeking through the night.
A blanket woven from the sky,
In this silence, spirits sigh.

Underneath the moon's soft gaze,
Wrapped in winter's sweet embrace.
Every heartbeat feels the glow,
Of a world transformed by snow.

Shadows of Frosted Pines

Tall pines dressed in icy sheen,
Guardians of the tranquil scene.
Shadows stretch beneath the light,
Whispers weave through day and night.

The forest breathes in crisp delight,
Branches catch the glow of white.
Every rustle, nature's song,
In this realm, we all belong.

Dappled rays through needles fall,
Echoes softly, nature's call.
Within these woods, the heart finds peace,
As frosty breaths swirl and cease.

Together, we roam these trails,
Where winter's charm never pales.
Frosted dreams in shadows dance,
In this beauty, we take a chance.

Echoes of a Frozen Dawn

Morning breaks with shimmering light,
A world transformed, pure delight.
Echoes whisper through the trees,
Awakening the frozen breeze.

Soft hues of pink and gold unfold,
Painting skies with strokes so bold.
Each ray glimmers on the snow,
Telling tales of night's soft glow.

As day emerges from night's grasp,
The chill brings forth a gentle rasp.
Nature stirs, begins to wake,
In this dawn, our spirits break.

Frozen stillness fades away,
As warmth begins to hold sway.
Echoes of the night depart,
Filling light within the heart.

Slumbering Landscapes in White

Blankets of snow, so soft and bright,
Fields lie still, wrapped in white.
Trees wear crowns of crystalline glow,
In this hush, time moves slow.

Footprints trace where dreams have fled,
Whispers held where sun once bled.
Gentle drifts dance with the breeze,
In winter's calm, hearts find ease.

Shadows stretch in the fading light,
Stars begin their silent flight.
Underneath the moon's soft beam,
The world sleeps, lost in dream.

Each flake a story, unique, sublime,
In this magic, we freeze time.
Nature's palette, so pure and bold,
In slumbering lands, beauty unfolds.

Crystalline Reverie

In a world where silence reigns,
Crystal visions break the chains.
Glistening shards reflect the night,
Dreams unfold in pure delight.

Frozen rivers softly glide,
Mirroring the starlit tide.
Every breath a frosty sigh,
Whispers of the winter sky.

Icicles hang like silent chimes,
Echoes caught in forgotten rhymes.
In this realms of mist and light,
Hearts awaken to the sight.

Time stands still in a trance-like haze,
Wrapped in a crystalline maze.
Nature's art, so vast, so true,
In this reverie, I dream of you.

The Whisper of Frozen Breezes

Through the trees, the breezes call,
A whispered song, so soft, so small.
Chill and warmth in soft embrace,
Nature shares her quiet grace.

Snowflakes twirl in the gentle air,
Painting stories everywhere.
Frosted whispers dance with glee,
A lullaby from the silent sea.

Branches sway in a rhythmic flow,
Carrying secrets only they know.
Each rustle tells of dreams that sigh,
Underneath the vast, cold sky.

In the heart of winter's night,
Hope ignites with a gentle light.
Frozen breezes bring a kiss,
In their whispers, find pure bliss.

Cloaked in Winter's Grasp

A landscape cloaked in winter's hue,
Every shadow, fresh and new.
Mountains high, draped in white,
Guard the dreams of the night.

Silent paths, where few have tread,
Whispers linger, softly said.
Nature sleeps, a perfect rest,
In her arms, we feel the best.

Stars like diamonds pierce the dark,
Guiding souls with a spark.
Frozen air, a breath so pure,
In winter's charm, we find allure.

Hope ignites in the snowy embrace,
In this wonder, we find our place.
Wrapped in dreams, we softly bask,
In the stillness, winter's grasp.

The Hug of Arctic Air

The chilly winds whisper soft,
Embracing the earth in their frosty grasp.
Nature's breath, crisp and aloof,
Wraps the world in a soothing clasp.

Icicles hang like crystal tears,
Glistening bright under the pale moon.
The silence echoes through the years,
A stillness that makes the heart swoon.

The stars twinkle, distant and bright,
While the air shimmers, alive with grace.
A ballet of shimmer in the night,
As the land drapes in winter's embrace.

With every gust, a fresh delight,
The Arctic's hug fills the soul with cheer.
In this frozen dance, pure and right,
We find tranquility, winter's near.

Boughs Burdened with White

Heavy with snow, the branches bow,
Each flake a whisper of winter's tale.
Nature's quilt, soft and somehow,
Blankets the world in a serene veil.

The trees stand tall, yet weighed with care,
Adorned in white, a delicate crown.
In the stillness, magic's in the air,
Their majesty wears a silvery gown.

Beneath the boughs, the silence reigns,
Footsteps muffled beneath the snow.
Winter's beauty, free of chains,
In every drift, a story to show.

As daylight fades, the shadows grow,
The landscape glows in twilight's embrace.
Boughs burdened with white, a gentle show,
Nature's beauty in the quiet space.

A Tapestry of Snow and Silence

A tapestry woven of white and grey,
Each flake a stitch in winter's design.
Where silence speaks in a magical way,
And peace unravels, soft and divine.

The fields lie draped in a soft, pure cloak,
Laughter of children, muffled yet near.
A world transformed, as if a joke,
Laughter frozen in moments sincere.

Footprints trace stories in sparkling snow,
Each step a memory gently laid.
Through this canvas, we wander slow,
In nature's embrace, our cares will fade.

A moment captured, a fleeting glance,
In the tapestry, we all are one.
Revel in winter's soft, quiet dance,
As day succumbs to the twilight's run.

Radiance in a Frosty Realm

In the frosty realm where the sun doth gleam,
Every surface twinkles like precious stones.
Nature's radiance, bright and supreme,
Illuminates the world with shimmering tones.

The trees, adorned with a silvery sheen,
Stand as guardians of this winter's light.
In their embrace, landscapes unseen,
Awaken to beauty, a pure delight.

Each breath taken is crisp as a bell,
Echoing nature's unyielding song.
In this frosty haven, we dwell,
Where moments of peace effortlessly belong.

As twilight falls and the sky ignites,
The stars awaken in a dance so grand.
In this frosty realm, we find new heights,
Radiant dreams cradle our hearts, so tanned.

Shrouds of Frost Along the Trail

Whispers of winter paint the trees,
Veils of white that dance with ease,
Footprints hidden, ghosts of the past,
Nature's silence, a spell so vast.

Branches arching with fragile grace,
In this chill, a peaceful space,
Frozen echoes, a soft refrain,
Each step felt is never in vain.

Misty breath, the air so still,
Glimmers spark on the icy hill,
Frosty shrouds, a blanket tight,
Cocooned in beauty, pure delight.

The path unfolds, a secret way,
Where dreams emerge in shades of gray,
With every heartbeat, every sigh,
The trail beckons beneath the sky.

The Secrets Beneath the Ice

Beneath the surface, stories sleep,
In frozen depths, the echoes creep,
Layers whisper, tales untold,
Of warmer days and nights of gold.

Crystals glisten in the sun's embrace,
Each fragment holds its own grace,
The water's heart beats strong and true,
Waiting for spring to break anew.

Secrets linger in chilly streams,
Wrapped in winter's silver dreams,
Memories trapped in a glassy dome,
Yearning for warmth, a place called home.

What lies below, a world confined,
Waiting for warmth to unwind,
In hushed tones, the ice will speak,
Of quiet moments that we seek.

The Tranquil Canvas of Frozen Dreams

A canvas white, serene and pure,
Painted skies, the winter's lure,
Brushstrokes soft on fields of snow,
Creating peace in the world below.

Underneath, the earth lies still,
Wrapped in slumber, against the chill,
Frozen dreams drift through the air,
A masterpiece, beyond compare.

Every flake, unique in form,
In chilly winds, they twist and swarm,
Nature's palette, hues of blue,
A frosty world, forever new.

As shadows stretch with fading light,
The tranquil canvas warms the night,
In winter's grip, we find our muse,
Comfort found in every hue.

The Quiet Road of Winter's Embrace

A winding path through frosty trees,
Where silence falls like gentle leaves,
Snowflakes dance with a soft ballet,
A tranquil road leads us away.

Shadows play on the ground below,
Quiet whispers in the winter's glow,
Nature holds its breath in peace,
As moments linger, a sweet release.

Footsteps crunch in the evening light,
Each step taken feels just right,
On this road, our troubles fade,
In winter's arms, our hearts are laid.

The evening comes, the stars ignite,
A haven found, our souls take flight,
With every turn, a magic space,
On the quiet road of winter's grace.

Glimpses of the Frosty Realm

Whispers dance on winter's breath,
As crystals twinkle in the light,
Each flake a tale of frosted dreams,
Floating softly through the night.

The trees stand tall in fragile grace,
Enveloped in their icy lace,
A world transformed in purest white,
A silent pause, a tranquil sight.

Footsteps crunch on powdered ground,
Echoes linger all around,
Glimpses of a realm so bright,
Where every heart feels pure delight.

Beneath the stars, the night unfolds,
With stories whispered, secrets told,
In this frosty, fleeting scene,
Magic lives where dreams convene.

The Chill of Resting Time

Time slows down in winter's grip,
As moments linger, softly sip,
The world wrapped in a calming chill,
A symphony of silence, still.

Beneath the cloak of starlit skies,
Where frosty winds hum night-time sighs,
Each breath a puff of icy air,
A gentle hush, a tranquil prayer.

The hearth aflame with golden glow,
Inviting warmth against the snow,
With every heartbeat, peace aligns,
In this place where solace shines.

Rest now, dear heart, let worries tread,
In dreams of snowflakes, softly spread,
For in this chill, the soul can find,
A quiet grace, a healing mind.

Soliloquy of Silent Nights

In the stillness of the night,
Thoughts unravel, take to flight,
Shadows dance beneath the moon,
Carrying whispers of a tune.

Crickets serenade the frost,
While echoes linger, never lost,
In the soft embrace of dark,
A symphony, a lingering spark.

The stars above in quiet rows,
Glisten bright, as cold wind blows,
Each twinkle tells a story spun,
A secret shared 'twixt moon and sun.

Embrace the silence, let it flow,
For in this hour, we come to know,
The beauty found in soft repose,
In nighttime's arms, the heart bestows.

Beneath the Frosted Sky

Beneath the skies of silver sheen,
A landscape draped in frosty bean,
The world adorned in nature's art,
Where every breath feels like a start.

Muffled sounds of winter's peace,
In cold embrace, the heart finds ease,
Each crystal glint, a spark divine,
A moment frozen, pure, and fine.

The air is crisp, the night is deep,
In chilly stillness, dreams we keep,
Underneath the vast expanse,
Hope awakens in a dance.

With each star shining from above,
We find our solace, feel the love,
Beneath the frost, our spirits soar,
Embracing all that's yet in store.

Celestial Dance of Snowflakes

In the night sky, they twirl down,
Spinning softly, like a crown.
Each one unique, a fleeting grace,
Whispers of winter, a soft embrace.

They blanket the earth, pure and white,
Covering the world, a lovely sight.
Glistening stars, in the moon's keen light,
A celestial dance, oh what delight!

Falling gently, from heavens high,
Creating magic, as they sigh.
In their descent, a story spun,
A tale of beauty just begun.

With every flake, a wish is cast,
Echoes of dreams from seasons past.
As they settle, soft and low,
Nature sings in the winter's glow.

Murmurs of the Winter Wind

The winter wind begins to wail,
Through the trees, a haunting tale.
It whispers secrets, soft and clear,
Bringing tales of yesteryear.

Fingers cold, it wraps around,
Caressing each branch, a gentle sound.
A lullaby of frosted nights,
Cradling dreams in silver lights.

It howls through valleys, sharp and bright,
Painting shadows in the light.
The world in hush, as if in prayer,
Listening close to the winter's air.

Yet in its song, a warmth we find,
A cozy hearth, the heart confined.
For in the chill, life's essence glows,
Murmurs of warmth in winter's throes.

The Warmth Within the Chill

Frosty breath upon the glass,
Yet in our hearts, a fire will last.
Under blankets, we find our peace,
In the chill, our love will increase.

Hot cocoa sipped by the fireside,
In sweet moments, we abide.
Laughter dances in the air,
Love and joy, we freely share.

Winter's grip may hold us tight,
But together, we face the night.
For every frost, there's warmth within,
A bond that never will grow thin.

So let the snow fall, let it gleam,
In every flake, a cozy dream.
Through winter's cold, we'll brave the day,
Finding warmth, come what may.

Frozen Time

Time stands still in winter's hold,
Moments frozen, stories told.
Each breath a cloud in the frosty air,
Captured in silence, everywhere.

Footsteps crunch on a snowy trail,
Echoes linger, a distant hail.
Nature pauses, a deep inhale,
In frozen time, we set our sail.

Icicles dangle, like crystal chimes,
Glistening bright, transcending rhymes.
The world is hushed, beneath a veil,
In this stillness, we shall prevail.

Let us cherish this fleeting muse,
In the quiet, we gently choose.
For in the freeze, a warmth shall grow,
A heartbeat's whisper, soft and slow.

Mellow Dreams

In twilight hours, the world slows down,
Dreams take flight, without a sound.
Under stars, our hopes collide,
Softly swaying, the night our guide.

Whispers drift on a gentle breeze,
Carrying visions among the trees.
In mellow hues, we find our way,
Chasing shadows at the close of day.

Each moment cherished, tenderly kept,
In the warmth of dreams, we gently slept.
Together we weave tales of light,
Creating magic beneath the night.

So let us wander through this realm,
Where love and dreams can overwhelm.
With every sigh, a spark ignites,
In our mellow dreams, we find new heights.

Milton Keynes UK
Ingram Content Group UK Ltd.
UKHW020741221124
451186UK00024B/224